AF519508

Proverbs for Daily Life

A 31-Day Devotional to Deepen Your Faith, Gain Understanding, and Live with God's Wisdom

Charles Spurgeon, Oswald Chambers,
John Owen, Jeremiah Burroughs

Published by
GRAPEVINE BOOKS

www.grapevinebooks.com
Delhi | Mumbai
email: grapevineindiapublishers@gmail.com

Ordering Information:
Quantity sales: Special discounts are available on quantity purchases
by corporations, associations, and others.
For details, reach out to the publisher.

First published by Grapevine India Publishers Pvt Ltd 2025
Copyright © Grapevine India Publishers Pvt Ltd 2025
All rights reserved

CONTENTS

CONTENTS

I

"Before destruction the heart of man is haughty." Proverbs 18:12

It is an old and common saying, that "coming events cast their shadows before them;" the wise man teaches us that a haughty heart is the prophetic prelude of evil. Pride is as safely the sign of destruction as the change of mercury in the weather-glass is the sign of rain; and far more infallibly so than that. When men have ridden the high horse, destruction has always overtaken them. Let David's aching heart show that there is an eclipse of a man's glory when he dotes upon his own greatness. 2 Sam. 24:10. See Nebuchadnezzar, the mighty builder of Babylon, creeping on the earth, devouring grass like oxen, until his nails had grown like bird's claws, and his hair like eagle's feathers. Dan. 4:33. Pride made the boaster a beast, as once before it made an angel a devil. God hates high looks, and never fails to bring them down. All the arrows of God are aimed at proud hearts. O Christian, is thine heart haughty this evening? For pride can get into the Christian's heart as well as into the sinner's; it can delude him into dreaming that he is "rich and increased in goods, and hath need of nothing." Art thou glorying in thy graces or thy talents? Art thou proud of thyself, that thou hast had holy frames and sweet experiences? Mark thee, reader, there is a destruction coming to thee also. Thy flaunting poppies of self-conceit will be pulled up by the roots, thy mushroom graces will wither in the burning heat, and thy self-sufficiency shall become as straw for the dunghill. If we forget to live at the foot of the cross in deepest lowliness of spirit, God will not forget to make us smart under his rod. A destruction will come to thee, O unduly exalted believer, the destruction of thy joys and of thy comforts, though there can be no destruction of thy soul. Wherefore, "He that glorieth, let him glory in the Lord."

2

"Before honour is humility." Proverbs 15:33

Humiliation of soul always brings a positive blessing with it. If we empty our hearts of self, God will fill them with his love. He who desires close communion with Christ should remember the word of the Lord, "To this man will I look, even to him that is poor and of a contrite spirit, and trembleth at my word." Stoop if you would climb to heaven. Do we not say of Jesus, "He descended that he might ascend?" So must you. You must grow downwards, that you may grow upwards; for the sweetest fellowship with heaven is to be had by humble souls, and by them alone. God will deny no blessing to a thoroughly humbled spirit. "Blessed are the poor in spirit: for theirs is the kingdom of heaven," with all its riches and treasures. The whole exchequer of God shall be made over by deed of gift to the soul which is humble enough to be able to receive it without growing proud because of it. God blesses us all up to the full measure and extremity of what it is safe for him to do. If you do not get a blessing, it is because it is not safe for you to have one. If our heavenly Father were to let your unhumbled spirit win a victory in his holy war, you would pilfer the crown for yourself, and meeting with a fresh enemy you would fall a victim; so that you are kept low for your own safety. When a man is sincerely humble, and never ventures to touch so much as a grain of the praise, there is scarcely any limit to what God will do for him. Humility makes us ready to be blessed by the God of all grace, and fits us to deal efficiently with our fellow men. True humility is a flower which will adorn any garden. This is a sauce with which you may season every dish of life, and you will find an improvement in every case. Whether it be prayer or praise, whether it be work or suffering, the genuine salt of humility cannot be used in excess.

3

"He that handleth a matter wisely shall find good: and whoso trusteth in the Lord, happy is he." (Proverbs 16:20)

Wisdom is man's true strength; and, under its guidance, he best accomplishes the ends of his being. Wisely handling the matter of life gives to man the richest enjoyment, and presents the noblest occupation for his powers; hence by it he finds good in the fullest sense. Without wisdom, man is as the wild ass's colt, running hither and thither, wasting strength which might be profitably employed. Wisdom is the compass by which man is to steer across the trackless waste of life; without it he is a derelict vessel, the sport of winds and waves. A man must be prudent in such a world as this, or he will find no good, but be betrayed into unnumbered ills. The pilgrim will sorely wound his feet among the briers of the wood of life if he does not pick his steps with the utmost caution. He who is in a wilderness infested with robber bands must handle matters wisely if he would journey safely. If, trained by the Great Teacher, we follow where he leads, we shall find good, even while in this dark abode; there are celestial fruits to be gathered this side of Eden's bowers, and songs of paradise to be sung amid the groves of earth. But where shall this wisdom be found? Many have dreamed of it, but have not possessed it. Where shall we learn it?

Let us listen to the voice of the Lord, for he hath declared the secret; he hath revealed to the sons of men wherein true wisdom lieth, and we have it in the text, "Whoso trusteth in the Lord, happy is he." The true way to handle a matter wisely is to trust in the Lord. This is the sure clue to the most intricate labyrinths of life; follow it and find eternal bliss. He who trusts in the Lord has a diploma for wisdom granted by inspiration: happy is he now, and happier shall he be above. Lord, in this sweet eventide walk with me in the garden, and teach me the wisdom of faith.

4

"Remove far from me vanity and lies." (Proverbs 30:8)

Here we have two great lessons—what to deprecate and what to supplicate. The happiest state of a Christian is the holiest state. As there is the most heat nearest to the sun, so there is the most happiness nearest to Christ. No Christian enjoys comfort when his eyes are fixed on vanity—he finds no satisfaction unless his soul is quickened in the ways of God. The world may win happiness elsewhere, but he cannot. I do not blame ungodly men for rushing to their pleasures. Why should I? Let them have their fill. That is all they have to enjoy. A converted wife who despaired of her husband was always very kind to him, for she said, "I fear that this is the only world in which he will be happy, and therefore I have made up my mind to make him as happy as I can in it." Christians must seek their delights in a higher sphere than the insipid frivolities or sinful enjoyments of the world. Vain pursuits are dangerous to renewed souls. We have heard of a philosopher who, while he looked up to the stars, fell into a pit; but how deeply do they fall who look down. Their fall is fatal. No Christian is safe when his soul is slothful, and his God is far from him. Every Christian is always safe as to the great matter of his standing in Christ, but he is not safe as regards his experience in holiness, and communion with Jesus in this life. Satan does not often attack a Christian who is living near to God. It is when the Christian departs from his God, becomes spiritually starved, and endeavours to feed on vanities, that the devil discovers his vantage hour. He may sometimes stand foot to foot with the child of God who is active in his Master's service, but the battle is generally short: he who slips as he goes down into the Valley of Humiliation, every time he takes a false step invites Apollyon to assail him. O for grace to walk humbly with our God!

5

"Whoso hearkeneth unto me shall dwell safely, and shall be quiet from fear of evil." (Proverbs 1:33)

Divine love is rendered conspicuous when it shines in the midst of judgments. Fair is that lone star which smiles through the rifts of the thunder clouds; bright is the oasis which blooms in the wilderness of sand; so fair and so bright is love in the midst of wrath. When the Israelites provoked the Most High by their continued idolatry, he punished them by withholding both dew and rain, so that their land was visited by a sore famine; but while he did this, he took care that his own chosen ones should be secure. If all other brooks are dry, yet shall there be one reserved for Elijah; and when that fails, God shall still preserve for him a place of sustenance; nay, not only so, the Lord had not simply one "Elijah," but he had a remnant according to the election of grace, who were hidden by fifties in a cave, and though the whole land was subject to famine, yet these fifties in the cave were fed, and fed from Ahab's table too by His faithful, God-fearing steward, Obadiah. Let us from this draw the inference, that come what may, God's people are safe. Let convulsions shake the solid earth, let the skies themselves be rent in twain, yet amid the wreck of worlds the believer shall be as secure as in the calmest hour of rest. If God cannot save his people under heaven, he will save them in heaven. If the world becomes too hot to hold them, then heaven shall be the place of their reception and their safety. Be ye then confident, when ye hear of wars, and rumours of wars. Let no agitation distress you, but be quiet from fear of evil. Whatsoever cometh upon the earth, you, beneath the broad wings of Jehovah, shall be secure. Stay yourself upon his promise; rest in his faithfulness, and bid defiance to the blackest future, for there is nothing in it direful for you. Your sole concern should be to show forth to the world the blessedness of hearkening to the voice of wisdom.

6

"He that watereth shall be watered also himself." (Proverbs 11:25)

We are here taught the great lesson, that to get, we must give; that to accumulate, we must scatter; that to make ourselves happy, we must make others happy; and that in order to become spiritually vigorous, we must seek the spiritual good of others. In watering others, we are ourselves watered. How? Our efforts to be useful, bring out our powers for usefulness. We have latent talents and dormant faculties, which are brought to light by exercise. Our strength for labour is hidden even from ourselves, until we venture forth to fight the Lord's battles, or to climb the mountains of difficulty. We do not know what tender sympathies we possess until we try to dry the widow's tears, and soothe the orphan's grief. We often find in attempting to teach others, that we gain instruction for ourselves. Oh, what gracious lessons some of us have learned at sick beds! We went to teach the Scriptures, we came away blushing that we knew so little of them. In our converse with poor saints, we are taught the way of God more perfectly for ourselves and get a deeper insight into divine truth. So that watering others makes us humble. We discover how much grace there is where we had not looked for it; and how much the poor saint may outstrip us in knowledge. Our own comfort is also increased by our working for others. We endeavour to cheer them, and the consolation gladdens our own heart. Like the two men in the snow; one chafed the other's limbs to keep him from dying, and in so doing kept his own blood in circulation, and saved his own life. The poor widow of Sarepta gave from her scanty store a supply for the prophet's wants, and from that day she never again knew what want was. Give then, and it shall be given unto you, good measure, pressed down, and running over.

7

"The conies are but a feeble folk, yet make they their houses in the rocks." (Proverbs 30:26)

Conscious of their own natural defencelessness, the conies resort to burrows in the rocks, and are secure from their enemies. My heart, be willing to gather a lesson from these feeble folk. Thou art as weak and as exposed to peril as the timid cony; be as wise to seek a shelter. My best security is within the munitions of an immutable Jehovah, where his unalterable promises stand like giant walls of rock. It will be well with thee, my heart, if thou canst always hide thyself in the bulwarks of his glorious attributes, all of which are guarantees of safety for those who put their trust in him. Blessed be the name of the Lord, I have so done, and have found myself like David in Adullam, safe from the cruelty of my enemy; I have not now to find out the blessedness of the man who puts his trust in the Lord, for long ago, when Satan and my sins pursued me, I fled to the cleft of the rock Christ Jesus, and in his riven side I found a delightful resting-place. My heart, run to him anew tonight, whatever thy present grief may be; Jesus feels for thee; Jesus consoles thee; Jesus will help thee. No monarch in his impregnable fortress is more secure than the cony in his rocky burrow. The master of ten thousand chariots is not one whit better protected than the little dweller in the mountain's cleft. In Jesus the weak are strong, and the defenceless safe; they could not be more strong if they were giants, or more safe if they were in heaven. Faith gives to men on earth the protection of the God of heaven. More they cannot need, and need not wish. The conies cannot build a castle, but they avail themselves of what is there already: I cannot make myself a refuge, but Jesus has provided it, his Father has given it, his Spirit has revealed it, and lo, again tonight I enter it, and am safe from every foe.

8

"Yet a little sleep, a little slumber, a little folding of the hands to sleep: so shall thy poverty come as one that travelleth; and thy want as an armed man." (Proverbs 24:33, 34)

The worst of sluggards only ask for a little slumber; they would be indignant if they were accused of thorough idleness. A little folding of the hands to sleep is all they crave, and they have a crowd of reasons to show that this indulgence is a very proper one. Yet by these littles the day ebbs out, and the time for labour is all gone, and the field is grown over with thorns. It is by little procrastinations that men ruin their souls. They have no intention to delay for years—a few months will bring the more convenient season—to-morrow if you will, they will attend to serious things; but the present hour is so occupied and altogether so unsuitable, that they beg to be excused. Like sands from an hour-glass, time passes, life is wasted by driblets, and seasons of grace lost by little slumbers. Oh, to be wise, to catch the flying hour, to use the moments on the wing! May the Lord teach us this sacred wisdom, for otherwise a poverty of the worst sort awaits us, eternal poverty which shall want even a drop of water, and beg for it in vain. Like a traveller steadily pursuing his journey, poverty overtakes the slothful, and ruin overthrows the undecided: each hour brings the dreaded pursuer nearer; he pauses not by the way, for he is on his master's business and must not tarry. As an armed man enters with authority and power, so shall want come to the idle, and death to the impenitent, and there will be no escape. O that men were wise be-times, and would seek diligently unto the Lord Jesus, or ere the solemn day shall dawn when it will be too late to plough and to sow, too late to repent and believe. In harvest, it is vain to lament that the seed time was neglected. As yet, faith and holy decision are timely. May we obtain them this night.

9

"Be thou diligent to know the state of thy flocks, and look well to thy herds." (Proverbs 27:23)

Every wise merchant will occasionally hold a stock-taking, when he will cast up his accounts, examine what he has on hand, and ascertain decisively whether his trade is prosperous or declining. Every man who is wise in the kingdom of heaven, will cry, "Search me, O God, and try me"; and he will frequently set apart special seasons for self-examination, to discover whether things are right between God and his soul. The God whom we worship is a great heart-searcher; and of old his servants knew him as "the Lord which searcheth the heart and trieth the reins of the children of men." Let me stir you up in his name to make diligent search and solemn trial of your state, lest you come short of the promised rest. That which every wise man does, that which God himself does with us all, I exhort you to do with yourself this evening. Let the oldest saint look well to the fundamentals of his piety, for grey heads may cover black hearts: and let not the young professor despise the word of warning, for the greenness of youth may be joined to the rottenness of hypocrisy. Every now and then a cedar falls into our midst. The enemy still continues to sow tares among the wheat. It is not my aim to introduce doubts and fears into your mind; nay, verily, but I shall hope the rather that the rough wind of self-examination may help to drive them away. It is not security, but carnal security, which we would kill; not confidence, but fleshly confidence, which we would overthrow; not peace, but false peace, which we would destroy. By the precious blood of Christ, which was not shed to make you a hypocrite, but that sincere souls might show forth his praise, I beseech you, search and look, lest at the last it be said of you, "Mene, Mene, Tekel: thou art weighed in the balances, and art found wanting."

10

"The lot is cast into the lap, but the whole disposing thereof is of the Lord." (Proverbs 16:33)

If the disposal of the lot is the Lord's whose is the arrangement of our whole life? If the simple casting of a lot is guided by him, how much more the events of our entire life—especially when we are told by our blessed Saviour: "The very hairs of your head are all numbered: not a sparrow falleth to the ground without your Father." It would bring a holy calm over your mind, dear friend, if you were always to remember this. It would so relieve your mind from anxiety, that you would be the better able to walk in patience, quiet, and cheerfulness as a Christian should. When a man is anxious he cannot pray with faith; when he is troubled about the world, he cannot serve his Master, his thoughts are serving himself. If you would "seek first the kingdom of God and his righteousness," all things would then be added unto you. You are meddling with Christ's business, and neglecting your own when you fret about your lot and circumstances. You have been trying "providing" work and forgetting that it is yours to obey. Be wise and attend to the obeying, and let Christ manage the providing. Come and survey your Father's storehouse, and ask whether he will let you starve while he has laid up so great an abundance in his garner? Look at his heart of mercy; see if that can ever prove unkind! Look at his inscrutable wisdom; see if that will ever be at fault. Above all, look up to Jesus Christ your Intercessor, and ask yourself, while he pleads, can your Father deal ungraciously with you? If he remembers even sparrows, will he forget one of the least of his poor children? "Cast thy burden upon the Lord, and he will sustain thee. He will never suffer the righteous to be moved."

My soul, rest happy in thy low estate,
Nor hope nor wish to be esteem'd or great;
To take the impress of the Will Divine,
Be that thy glory, and those riches thine.

II

"Where there is no revelation [or prophetic vision], the people cast off restraint ...." Proverbs 29:18

There is a difference between holding on to a principle and having a vision. A principle does not come from moral inspiration, but a vision does. People who are totally consumed with idealistic principles rarely do anything. A person's own idea of God and His attributes may actually be used to justify and rationalize his deliberate neglect of his duty. Jonah tried to excuse his disobedience by saying to God, ". . . I know that You are a gracious and merciful God, slow to anger and abundant in lovingkindness, One who relents from doing harm" (Jonah 4:2). I too may have the right idea of God and His attributes, but that may be the very reason why I do not do my duty. But wherever there is vision, there is also a life of honesty and integrity, because the vision gives me the moral incentive.

Our own idealistic principles may actually lull us into ruin. Examine yourself spiritually to see if you have vision, or only principles.

Ah, but a man's reach should exceed his grasp,
Or what's a heaven for?

"Where there is no revelation [or prophetic vision] . . ." Once we lose sight of God, we begin to be reckless. We cast off certain restraints from activities we know are wrong. We set prayer aside as well and cease having God's vision in the little things of life. We simply begin to act on our own initiative. If we are eating only out of our own hand, and doing things solely on our own initiative without expecting God to come in, we are on a downward path. We have lost the vision. Is our attitude today an attitude that flows from our vision of God? Are we expecting God to do greater things than He has ever done before? Is there a freshness and a vitality in our spiritual outlook?

12

"A word fitly spoken is like apples of gold in a setting of silver" (Proverbs 25:11).

When a person's heart is secretly trying to make excuses or find ways to make peace with continuing in sin and not killing it, then the situation is deadly serious.

Sometimes a person becomes convicted of his sin and instead of doing what he should do to kill it, he looks around for evidence to build a case that he's actually OK with God despite this, so nothing needs to be done. For example, he might start remembering all of his great experiences with God and all the things God has done for him. This is actually a good thing – in fact, it's something the Bible commands us to do. That was what David was doing when he said, "Let me meditate in my heart" (see Psalm 77) and remembered all the good that God had done to him in the past. This is what Paul tells us to do in 2 Corinthians 13:5. And so in itself this is a very good thing to do, especially in particular seasons such as times of trial or temptation. Do it for things like this and it will be like as Solomon said.

13

"And I have seen among the simple, I have perceived among the youths, a young man lacking sense" (Proverbs 7:7).

Solomon says a man who was enticed by a promiscuous woman is "among the simple" and that he was "a young man lacking sense". Why did he lack sense? Because "he does not know that it will cost him his life" (v23). He was unaware of the severity of the evil he was doing. And God, explaining why they ignored His attempts to get them to change their ways, says Israel "is like a dove, silly and without sense" (Hosea 7:11). They weren't aware of the sentence of guilt they were under. Would it have been possible for David to go so long without repenting of his sin if it hadn't deluded him so that he didn't see the clear violation of the law he was guilty of regarding Bathsheba? This is why Nathan the prophet had to reveal David's guilt through a parable that was supposedly about someone else – that's what was required to pierce the thick black cloud surrounding David's mind (see 2 Samuel 12). This is what evil desires in our heart always do. They confuse our minds so that we don't fully comprehend our own guilt, as well as doing all sorts of other things that reduce the amount of guilt we feel that I won't go into right now.

There are numerous ways sin uses to divert the mind away from understanding the true severity of the guilt of it. Sin's evil breath fogs up the mind so that it can't make a proper judgment about it. Rationalizations, extenuating circumstances, mixed-up desires, promises to reform later, and hope for future forgiveness all play a role in keeping the mind from truly understanding the magnitude of what we are doing.

Hosea tells us that sin will completely eradicate our sense of guilt if it fully has its way with us, listing the "whoredom, wine, and new wine, which take away the understanding" (Hosea 4:11). Just as sin has this effect fully in unbelievers, it's also working for the same end in believers.

14

"Surely I am too stupid to be a man. I have not the understanding of a man.I have not learned wisdom, nor have I knowledge of the Holy One." (Proverbs 30:2-4)

You should think about how little you actually know about God. You know enough to keep you in total humility, but even that is but a tiny fraction of what there is to know.

Who has ascended to heaven and come down? Who has gathered the wind in His fists?Who has wrapped up the waters in a garment? Who has established all the ends of the earth?What is His name, and what is His Son's name? Surely you know!

This is also something you can use to tear down the pride in your heart. What do you know of God? What a tiny fragment it is! How immense is His nature! Can you look without terror into the abyss of eternity? You can't stand the rays of His glory.

Keep your heart in continuous awe of the majesty of God. Remember that even the most spiritual people on Earth, the ones we think have the closest relationship with Him, still in this life don't know anything other than the smallest portion of what there is to know about our God. God reveals His actual name to Moses, yet everything of His glory that He manifested to Moses – "The Lord descended in the cloud and stood with him there, and proclaimed the name of the Lord. The Lord passed before him and proclaimed, 'The Lord, the Lord, a God merciful and gracious, slow to anger, and abounding in steadfast love and faithfulness'" (Exodus 34:5-6) – was ultimately no more than "seeing the back" of God (Exodus 33:23). Everything Moses saw and knew amounted to small and tiny pieces compared to the total perfection of God's glory. That's why the Apostle John wrote in a way that specifically included Moses when he said, "No one has ever seen God" (John 1:18). He also compared Moses to Christ in verse 17, saying "the law was given through Moses; grace and truth came through Jesus Christ." In other words, nobody, not even Moses, has ever seen God.

We talk about God all the time. We talk about His ways, His works, His plans, and His character. But the truth is, we just don't know that much about Him. Our thoughts, our meditations, and the things we say about Him are completely insufficient to express His actual glory and the true nature of His attributes.

15

"Surely I am too stupid to be a man. I have not the understanding of a man." (Proverbs 30:2).

We know so little of God because it is God we are trying to know. He's a being who has described Himself to us as someone who simply cannot be known. What else could He mean when He says that He is invisible, incomprehensible, and so on?

He tells us that we do not, and cannot, know Him as He is. Most of the progress we've made in understanding God is actually understanding what He is not rather than what He is. So when we say God is immortal, infinite, etc., we are really saying is that He is not like us since we are mortal, finite, and limited. That's why Paul gives his glorious description of God as He "who alone has immortality, who dwells in unapproachable light, whom no one has ever seen or can see" (1 Timothy 6:16). His light is so bright nothing can approach Him. He is not seen because He cannot be seen – because we cannot endure the sight of Him. The light of God, in whom there is no darkness, prevents access to Him by any creature whatsoever. We are so weak that we can't even look directly at the sun. How much less into the light and glory of God?

When considering these things, a wise man will confess that "I am too stupid to be a man" That is, he knows nothing of God, and so seems to know nothing at all about anything when he turns his mind to think about God and His ways and works.

16

"A good man is satisfied from himself." (Proverbs 14:14)

'I have learned, in whatsoever state I am, therewith to be content.' (Philippians 4:11)

This text contains a very timely cordial to revive the drooping spirits of the saints in these sad and sinking time. For the 'hour of temptation' has already come upon all the world to try the inhabitants of the earth. In particular, this is the day of Jacob's trouble in our own bowels.

How are we sufficient of ourselves! Our Apostle affirms in another case, 'That we are not sufficient of ourselves to think anything as of ourselves' (2 Corinthians 3:5).

Therefore his meaning must be, I find a sufficiency of satisfaction in my own heart, through the grace of Christ that is in me. Though I have not outward comforts and worldly conveniences to supply my necessities, yet I have a sufficient portion between Christ and my soul abundantly to satisfy me in every condition.

Because he had a right to the covenant and promise, which virtually contains everything, and an interest in Christ, the fountain and good of all, it is no marvel that he said that in whatsoever state he was in, he was content.

17

"In the house of the righteous is much treasure, but in the revenues of the wicked is trouble." (Proverbs 15:6)

Here is a Scripture to show that a gracious heart has cause to say that it is in a good condition, whatever it is. In the house of the righteous is much treasure; his house-what house? It may be a poor cottage, and perhaps he has scarcely a stool to sit on. Perhaps he is forced to sit on a stump of wood or part of a block instead of a stool, or perhaps he has scarcely a bed to lie on, or a dish to eat in.

Yet the Holy Ghost says, 'In the house of the righteous is much treasure.'

Let the righteous man be the poorest man in the world-it may be that someone has come and taken all the goods from out of his house for debt. Perhaps his house is plundered and all is gone; yet still, 'In the house of the righteous is much treasure.'

The righteous man can never be made so poor, to have his house so rifled and spoiled, but there will remain much treasure within. If he has but a dish or a spoon or anything in the world in his house, there will be much treasure so long as he is there. There is the presence of God and the blessing of God upon him, and therein is much treasure. But in the revenues of the wicked there is trouble. There is more treasure in the poorest body's house, if he is godly, than in the house of the greatest man in the world, who has his fine hangings and finely-wrought beds and chairs and couches and cupboards of plate and the like. Whatever he has, he has not so much treasure in it as there is in the house of the poorest righteous soul.

18

"Better is a little with righteousness than great revenues without right." (Proverbs 16:8).

A man who has but a little, yet if he has it with righteousness, it is better than a great deal without right, yea, better than the great revenues of the wicked- so you have it in another Scripture. That is the next thing in Christian contentment: the mystery is in this, that he lives on the dew of God's blessing, in all the good things that he enjoys.

Just as every affliction that the wicked have here is but the beginning of sorrows, and forerunner of those eternal sorrows that they are likely to have hereafter in Hell, so every comfort you have is a forerunner of those eternal mercies you shall have with God in Heaven.

Not only are the consolations of God's Spirit the forerunners of those eternal comforts you shall have in Heaven, but when you sit at your table, and rejoice with your wife and children and friends, you may look upon every one of those but as a forerunner, yea the very earnest penny of eternal life to you. Now if this is so, it is no marvel that a Christian is contented, but this is a mystery to the wicked.

I have what I have from the love of God, and I have it sanctified to me by God, and I have it free of cost from God by the purchase of the blood of Jesus Christ, and I have it as a forerunner of those eternal mercies that are reserved for me; and in this my soul rejoices. There is a secret dew of God's goodness and blessing upon him in his estate that others have not.

19

"A good man shall be satisfied from himself', from that which is within himself-that is the meaning." (Proverbs 14:14)

A gracious man has a bird within his own bosom which makes him melody enough, though he lacks music. A godly man not only makes up everything in God, but finds enough in himself to make up all-to make up everything in himself, not from himself, but in himself-and that may seem to be stranger than the other. To make up everything in God is something, nay, to make up everything in himself (not from himself but in himself)-a gracious heart has so much of God within himself, that he has enough there to make up all his outward wants.

20

"Wilt thou set thine eyes upon that which is not?" (Proverbs 23:5)

Why, blessed God, do not you do so? you have set your heart upon us and yet we are nothing. God would not have set our hearts upon riches, because they are nothing, and yet God is pleased to set his heart upon us, and we are nothing: that is God's grace, free grace, and therefore it does not much matter what I suffer, for I am as nothing.

I remember Bradford the martyr said, 'Whoever has not learned the lesson of the cross, has not learned his ABC in Christianity.' This is where Christ begins with his scholars, and those in the lowest form must begin with this; if you mean to be Christians at all, you must buckle to this or you can never be Christian.

He comes to this, to be able to say, 'Well, I see I am nothing in myself.' That man or woman who indeed knows that he or she is nothing, and has learned it thoroughly will be able to bear anything. The way to be able to bear anything is to know that we are nothing in ourselves.

21

"Faithful are the wounds of a friend." (Proverbs 27:6)

All great Christians have been wounded souls. It is strange what a wound will do to a man. Here's a soldier who goes out to the battlefield. He is full of jokes and strength and self-assurance; then one day a piece of shrapnel tears through him and he falls, a whimpering, beaten, defeated man. Suddenly his whole world collapses around him and this man, instead of being the great, strong, broad-chested fellow that he thought he was, suddenly becomes a whimpering boy again. And such have ever been known, I am told, to cry for their mothers when they lie bleeding and suffering on the field of battle. There is nothing like a wound to take the self-assurance out of us, to reduce us to childhood again and make us small and helpless in our own sight.

I don't know about you, but the only way I can keep right with God is to keep contrite, to keep a sense of contrition upon my spirit.

Now there's a lot of cheap and easy getting rid of sin and getting your repentance disposed of. But the great Christians, in and out of the Bible, have been those who were wounded with a sense of contrition so that they never quite got over the thought and the feeling that they personally had crucified Jesus. The great Bishop Usher each week used to go down by the riverbank and there all Saturday afternoon kneel by a log and bewail his sins before his God.

Perhaps that was the secret of his greatness.

22

"The patient man is better than the valiant; and he that ruleth his spirit, than he that taketh cities." Proverbs 16: 32.

O My God, when shall I be armed with patience as a shield against the weapons of my enemy? When shall I so love Thee as to receive with joy all the afflictions Thou shalt be pleased to send? O life of my soul, shall I never begin to live for Thy glory alone, perfectly resigned to all sufferings? O how happy should I be, if in the fiery trial of tribulation, I burn with a desire of being consumed for Thy service.

Let such prayers be offered frequently, as our devotion suggests, and our progress in virtue requires. They are called ejaculations, which like darts of fire directed to Heaven, lift our hearts heavenwards to the divine Goodness, when accompanied by two qualities which serve as wings: the one quality, a conviction of the delight God takes in seeing us labor for the cultivation of virtues; the other, an earnest desire of excelling in all virtue, for the sole motive of pleasing Him.

23

"Where there is no revelation [or prophetic vision], the people cast off restraint...." (Proverbs 29:18)

There is a difference between holding on to a principle and having a vision. A principle does not come from moral inspiration, but a vision does. People who are totally consumed with idealistic principles rarely do anything. A person's own idea of God and His attributes may actually be used to justify and rationalize his deliberate neglect of his duty. Jonah tried to excuse his disobedience by saying to God, ". . . I know that You are a gracious and merciful God, slow to anger and abundant in lovingkindness, One who relents from doing harm" (Jonah 4:2). I too may have the right idea of God and His attributes, but that may be the very reason why I do not do my duty. But wherever there is vision, there is also a life of honesty and integrity, because the vision gives me the moral incentive.

Our own idealistic principles may actually lull us into ruin. Examine yourself spiritually to see if you have vision, or only principles.

Ah, but a man's reach should exceed his grasp,

Or what's a heaven for?

"Where there is no revelation [or prophetic vision] . . ." Once we lose sight of God, we begin to be reckless. We cast off certain restraints from activities we know are wrong. We set prayer aside as well and cease having God's vision in the little things of life. We simply begin to act on our own initiative. If we are eating only out of our own hand, and doing things solely on our own initiative without expecting God to come in, we are on a downward path. We have lost the vision. Is our attitude today an attitude that flows from our vision of God? Are we expecting God to do greater things than He has ever done before? Is there a freshness and a vitality in our spiritual outlook?

24

"The liberal soul shall be made fat." (Proverbs 11:25)

If I desire to flourish in soul, I must not hoard up my stores but must distribute to the poor. To be close and niggardly is the world's way to prosperity, but it is not God's way, for He saith, "There is that scattereth, and yet increaseth; and there is that withholdeth more than is meet, and it tendeth to poverty." Faith's way of gaining is giving. I must try this again and again, and I may expect that as much of prosperity as will be good for me will come to me as a gracious reward for a liberal course of action.

Of course, I may not be sure of growing rich. I shall be fat but not too fat. Too great riches might make me as unwieldy as corpulent persons usually are and cause me the dyspepsia of worldliness, and perhaps bring on a fatty degeneration of the heart. No, if I am fat enough to be healthy, I may well be satisfied; and if the Lord grants me a competence, I may be thoroughly content.

But there is a mental and spiritual fatness which I would greatly covet, and this comes as the result of generous thoughts toward my God, His church, and my fellow men. Let me not stint, lest I starve my heart. Let me be bountiful and liberal, for so shall I be like my Lord. He gave Himself for me; shall I grudge Him anything?

25

"The lip of truth shall be established for ever; but a lying tongue is but for a moment." (Proverbs 12:19)

Truth wears well. Time tests it, but it right well endures the trial. If, then, I have spoken the truth and have for the present to suffer for it, I must be content to wait. If also I believe the truth of God and endeavor to declare it, I may meet with much opposition, but I need not fear, for ultimately the truth must prevail.

What a poor thing is the temporary triumph of falsehood! "A lying lip is but for a moment!" It is a mere gourd which comes up in a night and perishes in a night; and the greater its development the more manifest its decay. On the other hand, how worthy of an immortal being is the avowal and defense of that truth which can never change; the everlasting gospel, which is established in the immutable truth of an unchanging God! An old proverb saith, "He that speaks truth shames the devil." Assuredly he that speaks the truth of God will put to shame all the devils in hell and confound all the seed of the serpent which now hiss out their falsehoods.

O my heart, take care that thou be in all things on the side of truth, both in small things and great; but specially, on the side of Him by whom grace and truth have come among men!

26

"He blesseth the habitation of the just." (Proverbs 3:33)

He fears the Lord, and therefore he comes under the divine protection even as to the roof which covers himself and his family. His home is an abode of love, a school of holy training, and a place of heavenly light. In it there is a family altar where the name of the Lord is daily had in reverence. Therefore the Lord blesses his habitation. It may be a humble cottage or a lordly mansion; but the Lord's blessing comes because of the character of the inhabitant and not because of the size of the dwelling.

That house is most blest in which the master and mistress are God-fearing people; but a son or daughter or even a servant may bring a blessing on a whole household. The Lord often preserves, prospers, and provides for a family for the sake of one or two in it, who are "just" persons in His esteem, because His grace has made them so. Beloved, let us have Jesus for our constant guest even as the sisters of Bethany had, and then we shall be blessed indeed.

Let us look to it that in all things we are just—in our trade, in our judgment of others, in our treatment of neighbors, and in our own personal character. A just God cannot bless unjust transactions.

27

"The prayer of the upright is his delight." (Proverbs 15:8)

This is as good as a promise, for it declares a present fact, which will be the same throughout all ages. God takes great pleasure in the prayers of upright men; He even calls them His delight. Our first concern is to be upright. Neither bending this way nor that, continue upright: not crooked with policy, nor prostrate by yielding to evil, be you upright in strict integrity and straightforwardness. If we begin to shuffle and shift, we shall be left to shift for ourselves. If we try crooked ways, we shall find that we cannot pray, and if we pretend to do so, we shall find our prayers shut out of heaven.

Are we acting in a straight line and thus following out the Lord's revealed will? Then let us pray much and pray in faith. If our prayer is God's delight, let us not stint Him in that which gives Him pleasure. He does not consider the grammar of it, nor the metaphysics of it, nor the rhetoric of it; in all these men might despise it. He, as a Father, takes pleasure in the lispings of His own babes, the stammerings of His newborn sons and daughters. Should we not delight in prayer since the Lord delights in it? Let us make errands to the throne. The Lord finds us enough reasons for prayer, and we ought to thank Him that it is so.

28

"Then shalt thou walk in thy way of safety, and thy foot shall not stumble." (Proverbs 3:23)

That is to say, if we follow the ways of wisdom and holiness we shall be preserved in them. He who travels by daylight along the highway is under some protection. There is a way for every man, namely, his own proper calling in life, and if we devoutly walk therein in the fear of God He will preserve us from evil. We may not travel luxuriously, but we shall walk safely. We may not be able to run like young men, but we shall be able to walk like good men.

Our greatest danger lies in ourselves: our feeble foot is so sadly apt to stumble. Let us ask for more moral strength that our tendency to slip may be overcome. Some stumble because they do not see the stone in the way: divine grace enables us to perceive sin and so to avoid it. Let us plead this promise and trust in Him who upholds His chosen.

Alas! Our worst peril is our own carelessness, but against this the Lord Jesus has put us on our guard, saying, "Watch and pray."

Oh, for grace to walk this day without a single stumble! It is not enough that we do not actually fall; our cry should be that we may not make the smallest slip with out feet but may at the last adore Him "who is able to keep us from stumbling."

29

"When thou liest down, thou shalt not be afraid: yea, thou shalt lie down, and thy sleep shall be sweet." (Proverbs 3:24)

Is the reader likely to be confined for a while to the bed by sickness? Let him go upstairs without distress with this promise upon his heart—"When thou liest down, thou shalt not be afraid."

When we go to bed at night, let this word smooth our pillow. We cannot guard ourselves in sleep, but the Lord will keep us through the night. Those who lie down under the protection of the Lord are as secure as kings and queens in their palaces, and a great deal more so. If with our lying down there is a laying down of all cares and ambitions, we shall get refreshment out of our beds such as the anxious and covetous never find in theirs. Ill dreams shall be banished, or even if they come, we shall wipe out the impression of them, knowing that they are only dreams.

30

Be not afraid of sudden fear, neither of the desolation of the wicked, when it cometh. For the Lord shall be thy confidence, and shall keep thy foot from being taken. (Proverbs 3:25-26)

When God is abroad in judgments, He would not have His people alarmed. He has not come forth to harm but to defend the righteous.

He would have them manifest courage. We who enjoy the presence of God ought to display presence of mind. Since the Lord Himself may suddenly come, we ought not to be surprised at anything sudden. Serenity under the rush and roar of unexpected evils is a precious gift of divine love.

The Lord would have His chosen display discrimination so that they may see that the desolation of the wicked is not a real calamity to the universe. Sin alone is evil; the punishment which follows thereupon is as a preserving salt to keep society from putrefying. We should be far more shocked at the sin which deserves hell than at the hell which comes out of sin.

So, too, should the Lord's people exhibit great quietness of spirit. Satan and his serpent seed are full of all subtlety; but those who walk with God shall not be taken in their deceitful snares. Go on, believer in Jesus, and let the Lord be thy confidence.

31

"The desires of the righteous shall be granted." (Proverbs 10:24)

Because it is a righteous desire it is safe for God to grant it. It would be neither good for the man himself, nor for society at large, that such a promise should be made to the unrighteous. Let us keep the Lord's commands, and He will rightfully have respect to our desires.

When righteous men are left to desire unrighteous desires, they will not be granted to them. But then these are not their real desires; they are their wanderings or blunders, and it is well that they should be refused. Their gracious desires shall come before the Lord, and He will not say them nay.

Does the Lord deny us our requests for a time?

Let the promise for today encourage us to ask again. Has He denied us altogether?

We will thank Him still, for it always was our desire that He should deny us if He judged a denial to be best.

As to some things, we ask very boldly. Our chief desires are for holiness, usefulness, likeness to Christ, preparedness for heaven.

These are the desires of grace rather than of nature—the desires of the righteous man rather than of the mere man. God will not stint us in these things but will do for us exceeding abundantly. "Delight thy self also in the Lord, and he shall give thee the desires of thine heart." This day, my soul, ask largely!